GHO⟨
OF ⟨

Remnants ⟨

Carolyn Bauer SUPPLY ROOM AT CONGRESS JCT.

A RENAISSANCE HOUSE PUBLICATION

ISBN: 1-55838-095-7

RENAISSANCE HOUSE
A Division of Jende-Hagan, Inc.
541 Oak Street ~ P.O. Box 177
Frederick, CO 80530

Cover photo of Congress Junction
Courtesy Carolyn Bauer

10 9 8 7 6 5 4

WELCOME

Some of the "ghost" towns selected for this booklet never actually died. Tombstone, Jerome, and Bisbee were mining centers that now thrive on tourism. Other mining areas such as those near Crown King in the Bradshaw Mountains and Congress north of Wickenburg are enjoying new mining cycles. But the majority of the formerly prosperous towns have been abandoned to the sun and weather without the protection of an historic district designation. Much ghost town history and lore was passed down by word of mouth, growing grander with each telling. Glowing population estimates were exaggerated by town fathers to paint a rosy picture for would-be immigrants back East.

For newcomers to the state, the Arizona Office of Tourism in Phoenix is a good place to find basic information. There are many fine Chambers of Commerce sprinkled throughout the state such as in Wickenburg, where a smile and a helping hand are offered to travelers. Small, locally run museums are fine sources though their hours may be erratic. The Arizona Historical Society in Tucson (with branches in Phoenix, Yuma and Flagstaff) has excellent exhibits and is a tremendous resource for material on all aspects of early Arizona.

Some recommended additional sources:
The Bonanza Trail, Muriel Sibell Wolle
Ghost Towns of Arizona, James E. & Barbara H. Sherman
Arizona's Best Ghost Towns, Philip Varney
Ghosts of the Adobe Walls, Nell Murbarger
Captivity of the Oatman Girls, R.B. Stratton

Other books in the **Arizona Traveler** series of interest to the ghost town hunter are:
DISCOVER ARIZONA
BIRDS OF ARIZONA
GEMS & MINERALS OF ARIZONA
ARIZONA CACTUS
PARKS & MONUMENTS OF ARIZONA

Thanks to Joan Metzger and Heather Hatch of the Arizona Historical Society, Tucson Branch, for their friendly assistance with photo selection for this volume, and to Don Bufkin for his reading services. Special thanks to Helen Bauer for her unflappable desert navigation. This volume is for Frances L. Bauer and Gladys W. Corbett

Contents

Vaughn Reichelderfer

DRIVING TIPS

Arizona deserts are vast and ruggedly beautiful, but those very qualities can be the ghost town hunter's worst enemy. *Before* venturing into the wild, be prepared. Always travel with water; a gallon per person per day in non-glass containers is a good rule of thumb. Take along non-perishable food supplies. Leave an itinerary with someone. Many ghost towns see few visitors and it could be days before another person happens by. Take spare clothing for nights can be cold. Be sure you have a first aid kit with instructions.

Top off the gas tank at the last available station. Be sure all engine fluids are at safe levels, and belts and hoses are in good condition. Distances are deceiving; hilly terrain and relentless heat demand more of your engine. Always take a spare tire, jack, flashlight and flares. On long descents such as between Prescott and Jerome, use low gear instead of constant braking, so brakes don't burn. Watch for marked flood washes. Any low area is a potential wash in a rainstorm. Leave wash areas if weather is threatening. If your car breaks down, stay with it. If you must leave, put a visible note inside the car describing where you've gone.

When exploring old ruins, wear boots and watch your footing. Keep alert for rattlers; snakes often will be in old stone foundations and rocky hillsides such as those near Octave. Rattlesnakes love a cool, moist or shady spot during the midday heat.

Pay attention to No Trespassing signs--prospectors and miners often don't appreciate interest in their property. Stay out of old tunnels and away from shafts-- they are extremely dangerous. Little remains of Arizona's ghost towns due to weather, time and souvenir hunters. *Please* leave the sites as you find them.

Carolyn Bauer   PYTHIAN CASTLE

BISBEE - Cochise County

Gracious tree-lined streets curve around both tiny boarded up homes and huge, graceful brick structures teeming with activity in this pretty town. After driving through arid cattle country in far southeastern Arizona, a quick ascent then sharp drop into cool, verdant Bisbee is a pleasurable surprise. Named for Copper Queen shareholder Judge DeWitt Bisbee, the town is San Francisco-like, with turn of the century buildings clinging to the steep walls of Mule Pass Gulch. Lazy alley cats sun themselves on crumbling stone steps that zigzag downward between terraced buildings. Homes are stacked almost one atop the other, and as old timers used to say, "most any fellow with a chaw in his jaw can sit on his front porch and spit down the chimney of his neighbor's house."

Bisbee's steep streets are now paved, but in earlier days, dust or mud made slippery footing. When torrential rains hit the fledgling town, thick sheets of mud washed down the hillsides, uprooting buildings and vegetation. Early Bisbee burst to life in 1877 after three Army scouts stopped to camp in the cool gulch. Scout John Dunn found copper ore samples and grubstaked prospector George Warren, who staked claims in Mule Gulch. Warren had no trouble finding areas to stake, and he subsequently named the territory the Warren

5

Mining District. When word of the copper-rich region reached the eastern seaboard, investors and prospectors alike headed west.

One of the shrewd investors to scour the vicinity was Dr. James Douglas of the then small Phelps Dodge and Company. Douglas promptly bought up property in the Warren district and eventually merged the Copper Queen and Phelps Dodge companies into the huge Copper Queen Consolidated Mining Company.

Bisbee property became a precious commodity and canny businessmen made tidy profits in real estate. Jim Hoatson, a copper mine manager from Michigan, visited Bisbee on vacation in 1898. Astutely summing up the potential of the area, he went home to raise capital. Captain Hoatson returned with $550,000 and bought 15 prime acres west of Sacramento Hill. He dug a shaft and dubbed it the Irish Mag Mine, which ultimately produced a fantastic $15-million in dividends, and enabled Hoatson to live comfortably.

The region was originally worked by a financially and racially mixed group, but when prosperity hit, class divisions became distinct. Bisbee was soon known as "a white man's camp." Women were discriminated against with laws banning their employment as saloon entertainers or bartenders (Bisbee's raucous red light district aptly became known as Brewery Gulch.) Ambitious Orientals willing to do backbreaking work for paltry wages were ostracized and forced out of town. Mexicans were banned from working underground in the mines and labor unions flexed their muscles. Unions garnered national attention when members of the International Union of Mine, Mill and Smelter Workers struck in July 1917; 1,186 people were loaded into boxcars and "deported" into the desert.

As happened in Jerome, when Bisbee smelted its copper ore, the stinking fumes were toxic to plant life. Its green hillsides became barren but for a mantle of dark sulfur covering the soil. Before World War I, the grimy smelter was moved to Douglas. Nature eventually prevailed and the hills regenerated their plant life. Bisbee's perfect climate is responsible for the fresh, manicured appearance that lingers today. Copper mining has faded, but mine tours contribute to the town's robust tourist trade.

From Tombstone, Bisbee is a quick 30 mile drive south on U.S. 80. Many buildings are beautifully restored and the Queen Mine and Lavender Pit run daily tours. A late afternoon drink on the terrace of the Copper Queen Hotel is a must.

CHARLESTON, 1889

CHARLESTON - Cochise County

In 1879 Richard K. Gird, partner in the Tombstone Mining and Milling Company, chose Charleston on the San Pedro River as mill site for Tombstone's ore. Tombstone's new suburb soon established itself as one of the rowdiest towns of the southwest.

A good-natured freighter named Durkee, who hauled loads of bulging ore sacks from the Tombstone mines to the busy Charleston mill, was rewarded one prosperous year and decided to throw a bash (complete with saloon girls) for his fellow teamsters and miners. All weapons were checked at the door of the Charleston bar Durkee rented, and the party began. The barrels of liquor flowed like the nearby San Pedro. Gambling, dancing, and story telling as thick as the cigar smoke filled the barroom. The inevitable brawl spread like a brush fire, half of the men joining in just for fun. In a fight better than any B-western, men were thrown through railings and chairs were tossed against walls, splintering into kindling as they fell. Bleary-eyed whores screamed, ducking fists that swooshed pell mell past their lopsided ruby wigs. Bottles smashed over grinning miners' heads, splattering their stringy hair with aged, golden whiskey before they thunked to the barroom floor. But a fine time was had by all except maybe Durkee who ended up with huge bar bill--liquor *plus* repairs.

From Tombstone, head nine miles southwest on the dirt road to Charleston. Fading adobe ruins are still at the site, reached by wading the river. The BLM has recently acquired much of this land and will make it accessible to the public.

Sharon & Bill Panczner   MALACHITE ON COPPER

CHRISTMAS - Gila County

The Christmas, Arizona post office, founded within the still visible general store, was open from June 17, 1905 until March 30, 1935. During that time, thousands of holiday greetings were sent via Christmas with its unique postmark emblazoned on envelopes and packages. This little settlement in the Dripping Springs Mountains was a place of uncharacteristically non-violent contention between whites and Apaches. Problems started in 1878 when Dennis O'Brien and Bill Tweed made a copper claim. Another claim was staked by Dr. James Douglas in 1882. The white men realized the promise of their claims, but were thwarted in their attempts to extract the copper when it was discovered that their claims lay within the San Carlos Indian Reservation. Their hands legally tied, the frustrated prospectors tramped on.

The copper remained undisturbed until December 1902, when N.J. Mellor and George Crittenden discovered that the reservation boundary recently had been changed to exclude this mineral rich area. They rushed to the property and took up claims, naming the townsite for the day of their arrival--Christmas.

Soon the peaceful community claimed upwards of 1,000 residents. Christmas weathered cycles of prosperity and deficiency according to the fate of its copper. But as with many old mining towns, some folks hung on and Christmas is populated sporadically.

From Winkleman take Arizona 77 north nine miles. Christmas is near the highway. Some ruins are visible.

Carolyn Bauer   CLEATOR

CLEATOR - Yavapai County

Born as a siding on the Prescott and Eastern Railroad, Cleator originally had the curious name Turkey. Turkey was founded and owned by would-be rancher L.P. Nellis who dreamed of running cattle instead of being stuck inside his dark saloon. To his great fortune, former sailor James Patrick Cleator happened into the saloon one day. The men shared a drink or two, and Cleator so impressed Nellis that in only one day they became partners. Nellis signed over a portion of Turkey to Cleator, gratefully trading his saloon keeper's apron for dungarees and chaps. Nellis retreated to ranching and Cleator took charge of the little town.

Turkey was eventually renamed Cleator, both to recognize its new owner and to alleviate confusion in delivery of mail to a similarly named town. Cleator flourished as the mines opened, but the population peaked at an estimated 1,500 residents. Unfortunately throughout the late '20s and '30s, mining fell off, and mines folded as quickly as green gamblers playing high stakes poker. The final blow hit Cleator when the railroad discontinued service in 1933. Homes were carted off to new locations, and the abandoned mines were heavily scavenged for scrap metal. James Cleator, sole owner of the nearly defunct town, created a national sensation when he placed an ad in the *Arizona Republic* listing the town for sale. Despite much interest, no offers were made. When Cleator died in 1959, title to the town passed to his son.

From Interstate 17 take Exit 248 (Bumble Bee) and continue down the dirt road approximately nine miles northwest to Cleator.

Carolyn Bauer   CONGRESS JCT.

CONGRESS - Yavapai County

The Congress gold mine was discovered by Dennis May, but three years later it was purchased by Chicago promoter Diamond Joe Reynolds. After Diamond Joe's untimely death a short four years later, the mine was bought by four other gentlemen, including Mr. N.K. Fairbank who had earlier established the town of Fairbank near Tombstone. "Lower Town" Congress was home to common laborers, while "Mill Town" housed company employees, the mill, and the hospital. Like many early settlements on arid sites, Congress fell victim to fire in 1898 which wiped out most of Lower Town's businesses. Finding water in Congress was often as difficult as discovering gold. Residents' only source was a small spigot located near the company store. Fortunately most folks lived below the store and could roll their empty 50-gallon whiskey barrels uphill to the water spout. The return trip over crunching gravel was grueling.

Today little remains of Old Congress. The area is now owned by a private mining company. Red mill buildings and amber-hued ore dumps are easily visible from the main roadway. Heavy trucks rumble down the dusty route, proving that mining is thriving again near Congress. A few old frame buildings are also visible from the road, but barbed wire deters curiosity seekers.

Heading north through Congress Junction on U.S. 89 and Arizona 71 (north of Wickenburg), turn left over railroad tracks. Just past the tracks, follow the wooden Ghost Town Road sign. Congress is visible about 2-1/2 miles down the road.

CONTENTION CITY

CONTENTION CITY - Cochise County

Only a few dwindling adobe walls and a small cemetery mark Contention City, once home to three busy mills. The Grand Central, Head Center and The Contention mills clanked and clamored day and night processing thousands of tons of rich Tombstone ore. Contention City became a processing center, the San Pedro River providing a constant source of water for milling which was unavailable in Tombstone.

Miners and investors constantly inspected milled ore for precious metal grades, to assure that everything was still okay. Kinnears' and the Ohnesorgen & Walker stage lines daily shuttled businessmen and visitors from Tucson and Tombstone in and out of Contention City over tooth-jarring dusty roads.

Contention City boasted ten Anglo women who braved the frontier of the 1880s to be with their husbands. In fact, Contention City's population grew to about 200 residents in the short decade it existed. When its lifeblood of Tombstone ore trickled to a stop due to flooding in the mines, the use of the San Pedro sites for milling dwindled. Contention City's post office, opened in 1880, closed on November 26, 1888.

From the Fairbank post office, follow the dirt road running back through the fence for 2-3 miles. Contention City lies on the east side of the San Pedro River.

11

Stanley Zamonski

COURTLAND - Cochise County

It is nearly impossible to visualize the town of several thousand people that boomed here beginning in 1909. On the main street a steady stream of clanking milk wagons, businessmen's buggies and heavily loaded wagons creaked past horseless carriages. Hammers thudded day and night as carpenters threw up domino-style frame structures that were occupied even before they were finished. Two rail lines competed in servicing the region's four large copper mining companies-- Calumet & Arizona, Copper Queen, Leadville and Great Western. In later years, Courtland provided luxuries only dreamed of in other mining camps--a motion-picture theater, telephones and water mains. Two newspapers reported territorial politics and events. Though Courtland had high hopes of becoming a permanent city and acquiring the Cochise County seat, after a hectic decade the bloom was off the copper rush. Despite some flurries of activity, the slump had begun. Fortune-seekers, always scanning the horizon for the next storm of activity, were the first to leave. Businesses folded or were sold, and eventually most Courtland residents left. Some optimistic locals hung on, and the post office was operated until 1942. Today all that remain are two decaying frame and adobe buildings and a concrete jail--all an echo of the past.

Courtland is east of Tombstone on an unmarked dirt road, about three miles north of Gleeson but south of Pearce.

Arizona Historical Society ON THE ROAD TO CROWN KING

CROWN KING - Yavapai County

Anyone who has been jostled over the barely navigable route to Crown King will take pity on the pack animals that hauled loads of rich ore 40 miles over this hill country to Prescott. In 1904 the Prescott and Eastern Railroad conquered these mountains and ran fortunes in gold out of Crown King (earlier called Crowned King) back to Prescott. When the railroad ceased operation years later, drivers tackled high train trestles rather than the rocky hillsides.

Crown King gold was first found in the Bradshaws in the early 1870s. Known as Red Rock and then Buckeye, the name was changed permanently to Crown King when N.C. Sheckles and Co. held the town. Perhaps because of its seclusion, Crown King became a quiet little town. Company owners decided early to maintain order and not allow public drunkenness. As was true throughout the American West, much of the labor force around Crown King was Oriental and the little town had two Chinese restaurants. Surprisingly, this distant settlement had electricity and a phone.

Today there are geologists behind every rock in the Bradshaw Mountains, and old mine workings are springing to life again. The Bradshaws are home to one of the largest ghost town areas in the state. Crown King has year 'round residents as well as summer travelers.

Exit I-17 at #248 (Bumble Bee & Crown King.)
In a high clearance vehicle, continue past Cleator
about 12 miles west to Crown King.

Arizona Historical Society 1902 ORE DUMPER

DOS CABEZAS - Cochise County

Gold, silver and copper discoveries of the 1860s fueled Anglo intrusion into southwestern Arizona, home of the fierce Apaches. During Cochise's time, the Apaches used grim means to check trespassers, particularly in the Dos Cabezas and Chiricahua Mountains near present-day Dos Cabezas ("two heads").

Before the construction of protective Fort Bowie in 1862, Ewell Springs (later Dos Cabezas) was destroyed by Apaches. In a scant few years, 27 stage drivers were reported brutally murdered on the short route between Ewell Station (the first stop west of dreaded Apache Pass) and the fort. Eventually Apache aggression ceased and the Anglo population of Dos Cabezas soared to many hundred. The Central and Mascot copper companies thrived, and the town soon became a center for business and social activities. When a water table was discovered under the town, residents enjoyed an Arizona rarity--ready access to their own water supply. A bounty of copper was produced steadily until the mid-1920s when the vein was exhausted. To reduce taxes, swinging wrecking balls crashed through adobe and frame structures, leveling the Mascot Copper Company's headquarters. Soon few residents remained. Today Dos Cabezas has some full time citizens and mining era buildings, but no businesses.

From Willcox, take Arizona 186 southeast 14 miles.

Arizona Historical Society   EHRENBERG (ON THE COLORADO)

EHRENBERG - LaPaz County

Walking past gleaming racks of chic designer clothing in Arizona's modern Goldwater's stores, it is difficult to imagine the cramped and doubtless dusty adobe building that first housed the J. Goldwater & Bro. mercantile in Ehrenberg. Opened by Senator Barry M. Goldwater's grandfather, Michael, the store was established briefly in La Paz, six miles up river from Ehrenberg, but when the town floundered about 1869, Goldwater moved to energetic Ehrenberg where business thrived along the banks of the Colorado River. Before the railroad to Yuma was built in 1877, Ehrenberg was initially serviced by steamers grinding their way up and down the Colorado. For people with some means, life in Ehrenberg (while not always comfortable) was tolerable because the Colorado River provided an umbilical-like lifeline between burgeoning San Francisco and settlements downstream such as Ehrenberg.

Rather than spending hard-earned cash on Ehrenberg's imported "niceties," raw-boned miners preferred to dull their senses with a bottle of whiskey and one of Ehrenberg's plentiful, florid saloon girls. In fact there were so many saloons that when one faltered it became a makeshift school. Ehrenberg continued to bloom until the gold ran out and the new railroad choked life from the little river port.

Old Ehrenberg is two miles north of Ehrenberg on Interstate 10. A windblown cemetery and a few adobe walls are all that remain.

Carolyn Bauer   FAIRBANK POST OFFICE

FAIRBANK - Cochise County

Fairbank enjoyed prominence as a railroad siding and junction, as well as mail and supply point for the surrounding mining region. Wells Fargo shipped its treasures along the Fairbank route, prompting a sensational robbery attempt in February 1900 by a gang of desperados which included the Owens brothers and Three Fingered Jack Dunlap. The criminals jumped the Wells Fargo car, catching guard Jeff Milton by surprise. They shot him, shattering his arm. While lead balls whizzed by Milton, he managed to get off some shots, mortally wounding Three Fingered Jack, then tossed the treasure box key out the car door, foiling the robbery. Believing Milton dead, the bandits entered the car, realized the booty was unattainable, packed up Three Fingered Jack, and fled before the townspeople found them. They abandoned Jack in the desert where he was later found critically wounded. He confessed, implicating the others, and then died. Milton was rushed to San Francisco for surgery. When told that his arm would have to be amputated, he threatened to kill any doctor who did the job. He ultimately recovered-- with both arms intact.

Fairbank is six miles from the junction of Arizona 82 and U.S. 80. Turn right before the bridge. The abandoned adobe post office, a house and a commercial building are fascinating reminders of the past. Extremely easy access!

16

HOSPITAL FOREGROUND; JAIL BACKGROUND

GLEESON - Cochise County

Early Spaniards who penetrated southern Arizona mined semi-precious turquoise in the homeland of native Apaches. Spanish influence later subsided, and the Indians were left alone until whites intruded. Cochise and his tribe were a far cry from the early Apaches of the region, making the Dragoon Mountains impervious to nearly all Army assaults. For ten years the Apaches wreaked destruction on settlements in the region. One exception was Tom Jeffords, a mail contractor on the old Butterfield Stage line, who lost 22 men to the Apaches' wrath. Legend has it that in desperation, Jeffords rode alone to Cochise's hideout hoping to negotiate a separate peace with the chief. Cochise was greatly impressed with Jeffords' courage and they became friends and blood brothers. Jeffords later served as intermediary between Cochise and General Howard, and became Indian agent in the region.

When Cochise died, his burial spot was held sacred; Jeffords kept the grave's location secret for the rest of his life. Eventually the Apache uprisings ceased, and whites flooded the Dragoons looking for gold, silver, and bright turquoise. The town of Turquoise, later Gleeson, was founded, and Tiffany's of New York invested in the region, hoping to find a turquoise bonanza. Small strikes were made, but a large windfall evaded the company and it left. Gleeson faded, leaving only cattle and a few families to inhabit the site.

At the south end of Tombstone is a winding, dusty road heading 16 miles east to Gleeson. Modern residents forego adobe homes for trailers.

Arizona Historical Society GLOBE ATHLETES, c.1886

GLOBE - Gila County

Clanging, ponderous ox carts and long mule trains hauled copper ore down busy Broad Street in Globe more than 100 years ago. Globe's ore benches initially were mined only for their rich white silver; unsought copper ore was tossed aside. But about 1881, wise miners realized the potential of copper. The original copper processing furnace was built six miles from the Globe Ledge and Globe claims, but was later moved to the town of Globe by the Old Dominion Company.

Copper production thrived until 1886 when a number of factors made it uneconomical. First, the price of copper plummeted, removing mining incentive. Second, transporting ore was arduous and often hazardous. Copper had to be shipped by pack train over a grueling 120-mile stretch of desert to reach the nearest railhead at Willcox. A direct railroad out of Globe was a necessity, but the only practical access was across the San Carlos Indian Reservation. Apache/white relations had been strained for years, and the Apaches were hesitant to permit the intrusive railway.

To the relief of Globe residents, an agreement was reached. The Apaches settled for $8,000 in trinkets and were promised unlimited free access to the railroad for 30 years. The first train chugged into its new Globe siding December 1, 1898, and Globe again prospered. Despite greatly reduced operations, Globe lives on today.

> *Globe is adjacent to the San Carlos Indian Reservation in eastern Arizona. Take U.S. 60/89 east from Phoenix. At Florence Junction continue on U.S. 60 about 46 miles to Globe.*

Carolyn Bauer

GOLDFIELD, NEAR THE SUPERSTITION MOUNTAINS

GOLDFIELD - Pinal County

Goldfield once nestled at the western base of the soaring Superstition Mountains near present-day Apache Junction east of Phoenix. Like many other mining camps, it went through cycles of frantic activity followed by dormancy. Now it has died. As its name implies, the town was established following the discovery of a large, low-grade, gold ore body in 1892. Gold fever followed. Grizzled prospectors and soft-cheeked greenhorns raced to the town to stake over a dozen mines including the profitable Bluebird. Reverend Clarke, a wizened, itinerant minister, preached on Sunday in Goldfield's finest drinking establishment.

By 1897, the heyday was waning. In the early 1900s, Goldfield was revived as Youngsberg by George U. Young. Young hoped to raise recovery percentages by bringing in the latest mining technology--a cyanide plant and a thundering stamp mill. But this second boom cycle was also short-lived; the recovery costs of the low-grade ore simply outpaced the profits. Today there is a curio shop filled with mining and ghost town information next to a small display of rusting ore buckets. The rest of Goldfield has been razed, succumbing to new miners and heavy equipment.

From U.S. 60/89 take Apache Junction Rd. 4-1/2 miles north. The Goldfield monument is located before Lost Dutchman State Park turnoff.

Sharon & Bill Panczner   GOLD

GOLDROAD - Mohave County

Rumor has it that in 1899 while stalking his wandering burro, Jose Jerez happened upon a rich outcrop of
gold. Gold had been discovered in this region in 1863
by John Moss and some prospecting was done, but
little came of it. Prospectors subsequently abandoned
the region, considering it barren. But Jose Jerez knew
gold when he saw it, and became one of few Mexican
prospectors to make a good profit from his wanderings.
Jerez and his grubstaking partner, Henry Lovin, sold
their mine in 1901. The town of Acme (later renamed
Goldroad) popped up near his discovery. Though the
gold ore was low grade, production in the area continued for 30 years, yielding over $7 million for the
collective owners. Jerez dropped from the region's
history, reportedly committing suicide, but his partner
Lovin amassed a fortune with his prosperous Gold
Road Club and busy freighting company.

The area is littered with shaft and tunnel remains,
but as has happened with many Arizona mining towns,
buildings were purposely demolished (usually through
fire), to lower taxes. Today, Goldroad's best remains
are rock and adobe. Unfortunately, nature is already
melting the adobe buildings into the desert floor, and
soon only the rock construction will endure.

---

*Head southwest from Kingman on I-40, old
Route 66. Take Exit 44 into the Black Mountains.
Goldroad is approximately 25 miles from King-
man.*

Carolyn Bauer   SLIDING JAIL

JEROME - Yavapai County

When Jerome's policemen noticed concrete jail cells sliding away from the wood and tin sheriff's office, the jail was quickly deemed unsafe and their charges moved. And none too soon! The recently stabilized "Sliding Jail" has gradually skidded 225 feet down hill from its original location.

There are several reasons why the jail and other Jerome buildings have moved downhill over the years. First, the town is perched on a 30 degree slope on the side of Mingus Mountain, bisected by the Verde Fault. Second, underground springs have loosened soil, degrading its stability. Finally, in 1925 a huge explosion was detonated underground to facilitate copper mining. The plan was also successful in weakening the miles of underground tunneling, causing cave-ins and more sliding.

In the name of copper mining, Jerome has endured more than just sliding buildings. Heavy, stinking, sulfur-laden smoke billowed through the town from its earliest smelters, killing all but the hardiest plant life on Cleopatra Hill. Water in tunnels beneath the town mixed with loose minerals to form sulfuric acid. Health problems among miners became a reality for the companies and Jerome erected three hospitals to deal with these problems.

Long before the miners discovered the rich copper deposits, the early Indians used the brightly-hued, blue and green copper oxides for decoration. The Spanish had explored here in the late 1500s, but the first

Carolyn Bauer   SITE OF JEROME CRIBS

modern man to notice Jerome's mineral potential was
Indian scout Al Sieber. Unfortunately Sieber never
followed up his discovery, and never profited from the
huge copper bodies. Captain John Boyd followed
Sieber's find, and in 1876 he posted the first claim stake
in the region. Through a series of transactions, much of
Jerome's mining property fell to Arizona Territorial
Governor Frederick A. Tritle who brought in a finan-
cial partner, Eugene Jerome. Eugene, cousin of Jennie
Jerome, (mother of Winston Churchill) bought shares
in Tritle's floundering company with the prerequisite
that the town be named after him. Finally able to bring
in a small smelter, Tritle began to profit from his
venture. In 1883 he consolidated his property with that
of a group from Philadelphia, the partners calling
themselves the United Verde Copper Company.

Montana millionaire Senator William A. Clark
eventually leased, then purchased the property. Clark
invested over a million dollars developing his new
property and reaped vast rewards. He also built a
modern smelter on the plains below Jerome and
formed Clarkdale, a small community near his smelter.
On the mountain he constructed a huge bachelor hotel,
the Montana House, and a narrow-gauge railroad to
haul ore down to Clarkdale. But the copper baron
found numerous problems with underground mining
such as inextinguishable underground fires, collapsing
tunnels, and chemical hazards. In an effort to eliminate
them, United Verde in 1920 opened its sprawling open
pit mine.

22

Carolyn Bauer   LITTLE DAISY HOTEL

The phenomenal success of copper mining brought Jerome from a town of 400 to a tumultuous city of nearly 15,000 at its peak. "Rawhide" Jimmy Douglas was one of the lucky men to strike a vast deposit. Douglas eventually became a multi-millionaire during WWI from the profit on his Little Daisy Mine. On the hill between Jerome and the Clarkdale plains he built his graceful white adobe mansion. Today the Douglas Estate is an Arizona State Park. Mining implements such as a stamp mill have been set into its sprawling lawns. Just off the landscaped terrace, a picnic area overlooks the vast plains and scarlet-colored Oak Creek Canyon near Sedona. The interior has been restored down to its sterling silver commode fixtures. Original furniture, burnished to its former splendor, fills a bedroom; the small chemist's office is restocked; and a refurbished library beckons. New to the mansion is the specimen room filled with dazzling crystals and mineral samples, and a huge room displaying memorabilia from the copper baron era. The best overall view of Jerome is from the Douglas Estate. Major mining ended in the area in 1953.

Jerome is on U.S. Hwy. 89A. Driving from Prescott, use second gear on the downhill stretches into Jerome, for burning brakes are a frequent problem. Buildings such as the Powder Box Church (constructed of old powder boxes and stucco), the Little Daisy Hotel (best viewed from afar), and the Douglas Estate (small admission) should not be missed. The Jerome Historical Society offers self-guided walking tour maps.

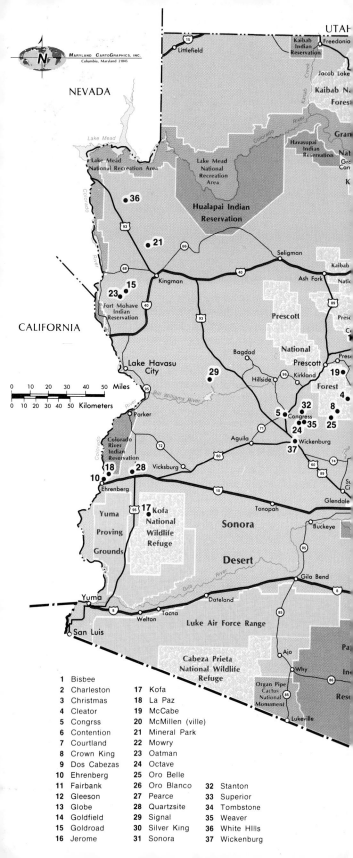

MARYLAND CARTOGRAPHICS, INC.
Columbia, Maryland 21045

NEVADA

UTAH

Littlefield

Freedonia

Kaibab Indian Reservation

Jacob Lake

Kaibab Na
Fores

Lake Mead

Lake Mead
National Recreation Area

Lake Mead
National
Recreation
Area

Havasupai Indian
Reservation

Gran

Nat
Gre
Can
K

● 36

● 21

● 15
● 23

Hualapai Indian
Reservation

Kingman

Seligman

Ash Fork

Kaibab

Natio

Prescott

Presc

CALIFORNIA

Fort Mohave
Indian
Reservation

Bagdad

National

Prescott

Presc

C
1

Lake Havasu
City

● 29

Hillside

Kirkland

● 19

● 4

Forest

0 10 20 30 40 50 Miles

0 10 20 30 40 50 Kilometers

Bill Williams River

Parker

● 5

● 32

● 8

● 35

● 24

● 25

Congress

● 37

Wickenburg

Colorado
River
Indian
Reservation

Aguila

● 72

Vicksburg

● 18

● 28

● 60

● 74

Su
Ci

● 10

Ehrenberg

● 17 Kofa
National
Wildlife
Refuge

Sonora

Tonopah

Glendale

Yuma
Proving
Grounds

Buckeye

● 85

Desert

Gila Bend

Yuma

Dateland

● 8

San Luis

Welton

Tacna

Luke Air Force Range

● 85

Cabeza Prieta
National Wildlife
Refuge

Ajo

Why

Pa

Ine

Res

● 86

Organ Pipe
Cactus
National
Monument

● 85

Lukeville

1 Bisbee	17 Kofa	
2 Charleston	18 La Paz	
3 Christmas	19 McCabe	
4 Cleator	20 McMillen (ville)	
5 Congrss	21 Mineral Park	
6 Contention	22 Mowry	
7 Courtland	23 Oatman	
8 Crown King	24 Octave	
9 Dos Cabezas	25 Oro Belle	
10 Ehrenberg	26 Oro Blanco	
11 Fairbank	27 Pearce	
12 Gleeson	28 Quartzsite	
13 Globe	29 Signal	32 Stanton
14 Goldfield	30 Silver King	33 Superior
15 Goldroad	31 Sonora	34 Tombstone
16 Jerome		35 Weaver
		36 White Hills
		37 Wickenburg

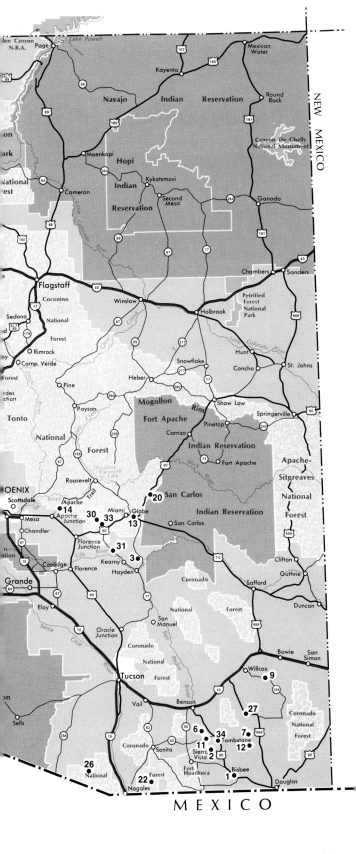

Don Bufkin   KOFA AREA

KOFA - Yuma County

Charles Eichelberger was wiser and luckier than other prospectors whose bleached and brittle bones littered the unforgiving desert floor during the Arizona gold and silver rushes. While prospecting through desolate Yuma County in 1896, Eichelberger wisely put aside visions of gold until he found a more precious commodity--water. The lucky prospector found a rock basin holding a puddle, filled his canteen, and rested. Peering across the thirsty land, he saw a towering, craggy butte rising from the flat. A shimmer of light on the dusty ground proved to be surface gold from Eichelberger's quickly christened King of Arizona Mine, its acronym soon given to the busy town that sprang up.

Remote and barren Kofa started fitfully. Timber and water were scarce, and worker accommodations were unknown. Miners without tents borrowed caves from irate rattlers or resorted to sleeping in the open. But Kofa's prosperity held and the weary miners were soon sleeping in real beds at the new boarding house. Soon a store, saloons, and a school were erected. An ethnic mixture of Chinese, Mexican, Cornish and Anglos made up the work force of 125 men. The King of Arizona mine built a 250-ton-per-day mill that churned out gold bullion until 1910 when the vein finally expired.

From Quartzsite, near I-10 and Arizona 95, go south on U.S. 95 for 28 miles. Go east 14 miles, then north eight miles to Kofa. Little remains to mark this old town. A dusty cemetery sits on the plain below Kofa Butte. Kofa is also accessible from U.S. 95 north of Yuma.

GOOD NEWS
FOR
MINERS.
NEW GOODS,
PROVISIONS, TOOLS,
CLOTHING, &c. &c.
GREAT BARGAINS!

JUST RECEIVED BY THE SUBSCRIBERS, AT THE LARGE TENT ON THE HILL,

A superior Lot of New, Valuable and most DESIRABLE GOODS for Miners and for residents also. Among them are the following:

STAPLE PROVISIONS AND STORES.

Pork, Flour, Bread, Beef, Hams, Mackerel, Sugar, Molasses, Coffee, Teas, Butter & Cheese, Pickles, Beans, Peas, Rice, Chocolate, Spices, Salt, Soap, Vinegar, &c.

EXTRA PROVISIONS AND STORES.

DESIRABLE GOODS FOR COMFORT AND HEALTH.

MINING TOOLS, &c.; BUILDING MATERIALS, &c.

SUPERIOR GOLD SCALES.   MEDICINE CHESTS, &c.

Original in Bancroft Library, Univ. of California

La Paz - LaPaz County

One of Arizona's favorite sons, Pauline Weaver, an enigmatic guide and explorer of the gold rush years, found rich placer gold lining dusty sands near the Colorado River in 1862. Weaver spread the news, then walked away leaving hoards to fight over the estimated 85,000 ounces of La Paz gold. After the gold was extracted with water, it was freighted overland. When Indian raids choked off this route, the miners began shipping their ores down the Colorado River to Mexico where the metals were refined and minted. Eventually the U.S. government put a stop to this outflow of gold by protecting overland shippers.

La Paz residents caught gold fever. Gold dust and large nuggets, or *chispas*, were used as cash; some even gambled with nuggets. Shrewd businessmen saw a bounty of wealth; the Goldwaters' first store opened in La Paz, to be joined by a brewer, a shipmaster, and a gardener. A heterogeneous town of Anglos, Mexicans, Indians, and a few white women evolved. Nature finally failed the settlement. During the spring of 1870, the Colorado River furrowed a new channel, leaving the little port less than a mile inland.

> *Six miles north of Ehrenberg on the Colorado River is the old site of La Paz. A decaying ghost town by 1891, La Paz today is a faded memory.*

Carolyn Bauer   DESERT AT McCABE

McCABE - Yavapai County

Like many early anglo settlements of Arizona, McCabe was, in the 1890s, a town of thin canvas tents, crumbling adobe boxes, and crude plank structures, all called homes. Water was a commodity as precious as gold, dairy products were scarce, and fresh fruits and vegetables were only dreams.

Overworked country doctors drove open carriages through blistering heat or pounding rain to sick or injured patients. When an epidemic of smallpox struck McCabe in May 1901, Mrs. James Broyles, a visitor from Ash Falls, was determined not to fall victim, although her brother, with whom she was staying, was stricken. Officials quarantined homes of the sick, trapping Mrs. Broyles in McCabe. When she protested, Mr. Broyles sneaked into McCabe at night and retrieved his wife. The next day the Broyles were caught strolling leisurely through Prescott and questioned about Mrs. Broyles' unapproved departure from McCabe. Her husband was fined $100, and both suffered the indignity of an intense spraying with liquid antiseptic. McCabe recovered from the epidemic and existed until 1913 when the McCabe mine closed.

From Prescott, take Arizona 69 past Humbolt. Go about four miles southeast past Humbolt via Iron King mine road to McCabe. A fire flattened the town. There is an old cemetery and tailings, but little else is left of the original town.

McMILLENVILLE, 1972

McMILLEN - Gila County

The silver camp of McMillen was born March 6, 1876 when prospectors Charles McMillen and Theodore H. Harris took a break on their travels between Globe and the White Mountains. Harris' chipping subsequently opened a rock laden with heavy silver, and the greenhorn abruptly wakened sourdough McMillen to verify the find. The men named their claim the Stonewall Jackson. Soon the area was filled with shacks, makeshift saloons, and men by the hundreds.

McMillen remained a male bastion, with few families settling the area. Life was rough and spare, but old-timers told of one glorious barroom Christmas tree, decorated miner-style with shiny whiskey bottles, plugs of tobacco, and crackling, aromatic cigars. Popcorn and cranberries were sparse, so miners strung the tree with fuse material and long shanks of dynamite.

The rich lode was tapped by eight mines and produced well into 1882. Ironically, in a region bereft of surface water, McMillen was hampered by underground water that filled the mines. The town flourished briefly, but declining silver prices and an Apache attack spelled its death. By 1885, it was just a memory.

From Globe, go east then north on U.S. 60 about 28 miles. To the east is the San Carlos Indian Reservation. Sparse mining remnants are left at the old townsite.

Thomas J. Barbre   "MUCKING THE TUNNEL"

MINERAL PARK - Mohave County

Mineral Park was known for its saloons, gambling halls and prostitutes ready to oblige miners and cowboys. Established in 1871 as a mining town, it prospered and in 1877 became the seat of Mohave County. This prized appointment brought additional jobs and stimulated an already bustling economy.

Nestled at the base of the mineral-rich Cerbat Mountains on Arizona's western flank, Mineral Park became a center for surrounding mining and ranching concerns. The town boasted a school, post office, weekly newspaper, restaurant, and hotel, the prevalent building material being adobe brick. Often an adobe building was plastered smooth and painted. Wise merchants erected a porch to provide shade from the blistering sun. Finally a false front of wood was constructed to give the building a two-story appearance and a large billboard.

Mineral Park outlived many mining camps, but eventually it faded from prominence; the post office was discontinued June 15, 1912. Modern mining companies thrive throughout the area. A fine cemetery lies hidden in the cholla.

From Kingman, go about 29 miles north on U.S. 93 to Chloride. Drop south six miles then east four miles to Mineral Park.

Don Bufkin   RUINS AT MOWRY

MOWRY - Santa Cruz County

Most evidence indicates that Mexicans were the founders of the Patagonia mine, later known as the Mowry. In 1860 Lt. Sylvester Mowry, a U.S. Army officer, bought the operation, renaming it for himself. Lieutenant Mowry did well extracting heavy silver and lead ore from his mine. But on July 2, 1862 he was arrested by General James H. Carleton and charged with selling lead for ammunition production to the Confederate Army. His mining property was seized and he was incarcerated at the dreaded Fort Yuma stockade. Mowry was released from prison on November 8, 1862, when no evidence was found to support treason claims against him. During his imprisonment, the Mowry mine had been sold, leaving him a poor man. Mowry left Arizona for England, hoping to obtain financing to restart his mining venture. But before that materialized, he had died in Europe in 1871, still unprosperous.

The Mowry mine's troubles didn't end with the death of its namesake. The wily, tough Apaches of southeastern Arizona were a serious match for any white men venturing into their homelands. When the region quieted many years later, a new interest bought the mine and the reborn Mowry prospered a decade into the 20th century.

From Nogales, take Arizona 82 northeast for 19 miles to Patagonia. From there, take the dirt road southeast for about 14 miles.

Arizona Office of Tourism   OATMAN/GOLDROAD AREA

OATMAN - Mohave County

Many an eastern family fell victim to dehydration, illness or Indian attack on the way west. The Oatmans were just such a family. Traveling west in 1851, they were attacked by Tonto Apaches (Yavapai Indians) near Gila Bend. Mr. and Mrs. Oatman were beaten to death with clubs, their son Lorenzo was beaten into unconsciousness and left for dead, and four other children were murdered. Two surviving Oatman daughters, Olive and Mary Ann, were spared and taken captive.

Mary Ann and Olive suffered abuse and deprivation under the Apaches and were eventually traded to the Mohave who were somewhat less cruel. But the Mohave suffered a year of bad crops and Mary Ann was among those who starved to death. Sister Olive (known as Ollie) survived and was held captive a total of five years. When Olive was about 20 she was found, traded, and returned with a permanent chin tattoo to her brother who had survived the brutal assault five years before. Olive married John Fairchild in 1865 and lived another 38 years.

The town of Oatman, named for the family, sits amidst a wild collection of craggy buttes. It was established around the turn of the century with the discovery of the Vivian Mine. When the Tom Reed mine was discovered in 1908, over $13 million in gold was extracted, and the town boomed. A third evolution began in 1913 with the opening of the United Eastern mine. Today Oatman's population see-saws according to tourism and volatile metals prices.

Oatman is about two miles south from Goldroad. A small town remains.

Carolyn Bauer   POWDER HOUSE

OCTAVE -Yavapai County

Today's travelers to the site of Octave will have trouble believing that the few stone ruins, concrete foundations and tailing dumps speckling the rocky landscape were once part of a town of 3,000 people. The name "Rich Hill" brought prospectors racing to the region in hopes of establishing yet another lucrative placer mine. Eight Pennsylvania oil men staked claims in the area (thus the name Octave), to form the Octave Gold Mining Co. By introducing modern recovery processes, the owners were able to retrieve some $2-million in gold from their claims.

Lode or shaft mining, not placering, produced the greatest wealth in this small region, best known for its profitable placer operations. Later purchased by ASARCO, Inc., the Octave bloomed again and is said to have produced well over $4-million in gold during its lifetime. Unfortunately, the town's buildings were razed to reduce taxes and not much remains of Octave.

Just northeast of Congress Junction (17 miles north of Wickenburg) is a sign to the Rich Hill District (Stanton, Octave and Weaver.) Go about one mile past Stanton. A stone powderhouse can be seen off the road to the left. There are a few other stone foundations down the road just beyond the powderhouse. Watch for rattlesnakes!

Sharon & Bill Panczner   GOLD

ORO BELLE - Yavapai County

Oro Bell's history speaks most often of two men, George P. Harrington and a man called Schlesinger. The former was a kindly mine manager who continuously grubstaked and employed needy miners--with company funds. When stockholders got wind of his philanthropy, they demanded a new manager who could stretch a dollar. What they got was a penny-pinching mining engineer named Schlesinger who cut all the fat from the bone, figuratively and literally. Paltry wages and wretched food, unfit for hardworking miners, were the order of the day. The men revolted, but Schlesinger soon resumed his brand of spartan living. This time the grim men threatened him into resigning. Smooth labor relations resumed only when the affable Mr. Harrington regained his title of mine manager.

The post office, established in 1904 under the name Harrington, was later changed to Oro Belle. The successful Oro Belle and Gray Eagle lodes, along with the nominal Rapid Transit and Savoy mines, employed 100 men during their peaks, and the town claimed 200 residents. Unfortunately the rocky Bradshaw Mountains were fickle with fortune seekers and Oro Belle's good ores were exhausted by 1910. Some rugged miners hung on until 1918 when the post office was permanently discontinued.

Oro Belle, now owned by the Arizona Historical Society, is about three miles southwest from Crown King.

Kendal Atchison   ARRASTRAS

ORO BLANCO - Santa Cruz County

A short distance from the Arizona/Mexico border
and just south of Arivaca is sleepy little Oro Blanco.
The original town was a small camp that grew from the
nearby Oro Blanco mine and blossomed in 1873 when
the mine was reopened by a handful of miners. It
survived about 20 years while workers extracted silver
or "white ore" from the ground.

Silver was taken from the natural ores by use of
seven "arrastras" in the area. Ores were placed in the
bottom of the arrastra, and a heavy stone or other
weight was placed on top. The stone was dragged
around and around the basin until the ore was ground.
Water was then run through it, washing out lighter
particles and allowing heavier silver pieces to settle to
the bottom. Most arrastra stones were powered by
animals, but occasionally human muscle was pressed
into service. Arrastras require an abundant water
supply, so were not a common extraction tool in
Arizona. But nearby Oro Blanco Creek provided the
water needed by miners in the Oro Blanco district.

The success of the Oro Blanco mine prompted
companies like the Orion Silver and Esperango to join
the fray, and soon two steam mills were operating day
and night. Oro Blanco's population jumped to about
225. Education was a priority, but the schoolhouse
wasn't--the children studied in a three-sided, brush-
roofed shack. Unlike many Arizona ghost towns, Oro
Blanco buildings are being preserved by the Noon
family, descendants of an original settler.

*The old town site of Oro Blanco is now located
on private property within the boundaries of the
Oro Blanco Ranch. It is not open to the public.
Please respect the NO TRESPASSING signs.*

DAVE DREW'S BUTCHER SHOP

PEARCE - Cochise County

Robust Jimmie Pearce and his sturdy wife "Ma" were typical of the hardworking Cornishmen and women laboring in the West's gold and silver camps. But the Pearces actually realized the dream sought by so many of their English countrymen. Early on the Pearces lived in Tombstone where Jimmie worked as a hardrock miner and Ma ran a boarding house. When mining around Tombstone fell off, the frugal Pearces gathered their savings and their iron wills and bought a ranch in nearby Sulphur Springs Valley.

Luck smiled on them in 1894 when Jimmie found a piece of gold-bearing quartz. He named his find the Commonwealth, and promptly staked five claims--one per family member. News of the gold strike spread, and soon flocks of acquisitive promoters hovered around the Pearces like hungry vultures. Pearce finally struck a deal with John Brockman, a New Mexico banker, which paid the Pearces $250,000--a whopping $50,000 per family member. But ever industrious, thrifty Ma required the new owners to give her a monopoly on running the new boarding house for the mine. The town of Pearce, formed around the mine, prospered into the 1930s. Today there are several buildings, including a former post office and museum, but few people.

From Willcox on I-10, go southwest 8 miles to exit 331 (U.S. 666), then south 20 miles to Pearce.

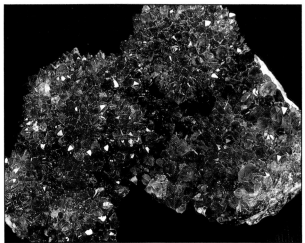

Sharon & Bill Panczner   AMETHYST, A VARIETY OF QUARTZ

QUARTZSITE - LaPaz County

More than one prospector choked on his morning coffee at sight of a huge, gangly camel lumbering across the desert near the stage station of Quartzsite. With the blessing of the War Department in 1856, two herds of camels (numbering 33 and 47 respectively) were imported from Tunis, Egypt and Smyrna. The stubborn, willful camels were used to help open a wilderness road from the Colorado River to Fort Defiance through dangerous terrain. Arabs employed to manage the animals soon left to find easier work, but one driver--Hadjii Ali, known as Hi Jolly--steadfastly remained.

Hi Jolly's camels were intractable but they carried much heavier loads than mules or oxen. Their awkward gait and towering height frightened smaller stock, however, causing stampedes. This combined with obstinate natures, an uncomfortable ride, and the onset of the Civil War cut short the camel experiment. The animals were abandoned to the desert. Many died of neglect and others were killed by a shot from a prospector or hunter. For years, many of the beasts were seen wandering across the lonely moonlit desert. Indian legend tells of one camel defying the gods of lightning and thunder and being turned to rock. She is known today as Camelback Mountain near Scottsdale.

Quartzsite is near the intersection of U.S. 95 and I-10 (and U.S. 60/70.) In the Quartzsite cemetery is a camel-topped, pyramidal monument dedicated to camel driver Hi Jolly.

Arizona Historical Society   UNION SUNDAY SCHOOL, 1916-17

SIGNAL - Mohave County

Visions of a second Comstock lured miners, investors and families to this isolated piece of desert in 1874. For the earliest inhabitants of Signal, life was a struggle. Goods were shipped by rail from California to the Colorado River, then along the river by boat, and finally on pack animals.

As the McCracken and Signal mines began extracting silver chlorides, processing mills were built, and prosperity took hold. Families, professionals, and rag tag crews of miners choked the streets of Signal. The peak population of 800 included many children. Schools, saloons and even a brewery were swiftly constructed; main street was stuffed with wood plank, false front buildings and squat adobes. Nearly 200 buildings speckled the dusty land.

Mercantile owners, wise to the supply time, were soon ordering goods six months in advance. A hard-working miner's wage was $2.50-$4.00 per day. Fresh milk and butter were available but were sparingly consumed at $1.00 per gallon and $1.50 per pound. When the initial rush receded, approximately 300 people were left in Signal. The mills continued to extract silver from the McCracken mine, at one point churning out $150,000 per month. The silver eventually gave out, and prosperity faded with dropping ore grades and prices. Signal residents tenaciously clung to their declining town, managing to keep the post office open until 1932. The area is now inhabited primarily by desert animals and cattle.

From Wickenburg, go 59 miles north on U.S. 93. Take dirt road south 12 miles to Signal. Mill foundations, a wonderful cemetery, and the old Signal Bar remain at the site.

Carolyn Bauer   SILVER KING MINING COUNTRY

SILVER KING - Pinal County

Two soldiers, elated to be dismissed from military service in 1872, lit out for the town of Florence on the San Pedro River. Along the dusty trail, ex-soldier Sullivan picked up several lumps of heavy black rock and tried to smash them. To his surprise, the rocks simply flattened, suggesting the rock contained malleable silver. Sullivan showed a sample to a friend, Charles G. Mason, but left without revealing the location of his find. Mason determined the material was mainly chloride of silver, but was unable to locate the vein until 1875 when he was riding through the area with three friends. On a rise covered with rocks identical to Sullivan's, the men founded the Silver King Mine.

Eventually the four partners sold their shares, the last for a princely $300,000. Sullivan returned years later, having saved enough money to work his find, but found instead a thriving mine and town on the very spot of his discovery. He settled for a job in the silver mill. The $17-million of silver brought out of the Silver King mine excited more than the region's bankers. Highwaymen were soon robbing the stage of silver bars shipped from the Pinal City smelter. To prevent such theft, the smelters began pouring the silver into bars so heavy that neither man nor mule could carry them.

From Superior, take the dirt road about five miles northwest to Silver King.

Carolyn Bauer   OPEN PIT COPPER MINE

SONORA - Pinal County

Mighty earthmovers working the rolling mountainsides near former Sonora expose veins of purple, crimson, mauve and gold. Where Sonora once stood quietly in the sage, there is now a clamorous open pit copper mining operation. Both Ray Mining and the Hercules Copper companies operated in the developing area during the 1880s, and the town of Ray bustled with Mexican employees. Neighboring towns such as Americatown, Boyd Heights, Barcelona and Sonora soon sprang up. Like many immigrant groups, the Mexicans of Barcelona and Sonora named their towns for their homeland.

The early copper companies eventually flourished, but over the years machines have replaced human laborers. Some still work the region's open pits and live near the moist river bed to the south or in the little town of Kelvin. The immediate area, once filled with bounding jack rabbits and yelping coyotes, is still except for the relentless noise of automated mining. The old towns have been razed to allow open pit mining, and the mines are surrounded by fences and gates.

The huge Bay Mine and the early site of Sonora are on Arizona 177 just north of Kelvin. The Bay Mine provides highway overlooks for viewing its operations.

Carolyn Bauer   STANTON HOTEL

STANTON - Yavapai County

Some of Arizona's finest remaining mining-era buildings are in Stanton, now a privately owned prospecting club known as the Lost Dutchman Mining Association. Members visit the "town" to prospect. The grounds are private, but the Hotel Stanton is visible from the adjacent public road. Stanton, originally called Antelope Station, was first populated by full-time prospectors and miners. Charles P. Stanton, a corrupt and vicious man, was often suspected in a murder or disappearance. It was Stanton who forced the town's affable stage agent and store owner, Barney Martin, to sell his properties. Cash in hand, Martin and his family headed for Phoenix, notifying a friend that they would be stopping at his ranch on their way. When, after several days, the family hadn't arrived, a search party was dispatched and found the Martins' burned bodies and wagon. Stanton and the notorious Valenzuela gang were charged in the murders, but no conclusive evidence was found.

Stanton finally went too far when he insulted the sister of a local tough named Cristo Lucero. Enraged, Lucero shot Stanton as he sat in his own store, and then hastily headed toward Mexico. On the trail he met a neighbor who advised him, "Stick around, you'll get a reward."

From Congress Junction, go about 1/2 mile east on U.S. 89 to the Stanton/Rich Hill road. Take this dirt road about seven miles until it crosses a concrete bridge. The first road on the left leads into privately-owned Stanton.

Carolyn Bauer

SUPERIOR - Pinal County

From the summit of 4,875-foot Pinal Pass, a ruggedly beautiful panorama reveals a cactus-dotted, pastel desert pierced by jagged, dark mountains stabbing at the cobalt sky. At the foot of the pass sits Superior, once an energetic town of several thousand. Today's Superior languishes drowsily in the desert heat. Many silent, boarded-up buildings line streets that once were clogged with traffic from the nearby Silver King and Silver Queen mines. The rich Silver King, discovered in 1875, brought an influx of money and people to the isolated area. On its heels came the discovery of the fickle Silver Queen. The Queen's tempting silver cap played out, discouraging many fortune seekers, but beneath her cap she hid another fortune in copper.

The Magma Copper Company formed in 1910 to exploit the deposits of the Silver Queen. In 1924 the company built a huge smelter to process copper from the Silver Queen and neighboring operations. Superior's rich copper production during the mining slump of 1929-1933 kept the town healthy, unlike many other districts. Today many abandoned ghost towns surround Superior, which is not a ghost town itself but an interesting mining center.

From Phoenix/Mesa take U.S. 60/89 east toward Florence Junction. From Florence Junction continue east on U.S. 60 to Superior. The Boyce Thompson Southwestern Arboretum is just 15 miles down U.S. 60 toward Florence Junction.

Carolyn Bauer   OK CORRAL

TOMBSTONE - Cochise County

A short 60 seconds and 30 shots after the fight began, dust and burning gunpowder settled around the motionless bodies of Tom and Frank McLowery (McLaury). Mortally wounded cohort Billy Clanton lived an agonizing 30 minutes longer, succumbing to slugs in his wrist, waist and chest. His uninjured brother Ike quickly fled the scene.

On the other side of the shootout, Marshal Earp took a ball in his right leg, while brother Morgan was hit in both shoulders. The wounded but fortunate Earps eventually recovered. Their luckier brother Wyatt and friend Doc Holliday remained unscathed. The deadly gunfight at the OK Corral sprang from a growing feud between the rival groups. When Marshal Virgil Earp sensed trouble and tried disarming the McLowerys and Clantons, the fray erupted. The dead men were considered by some to be drunken cowboys, and many locals sided heavily with the Earp fraternity.

This notorious gunfight occurred on October 26, 1881, during the early silver boom days of Tombstone. Prospector Ed Schieffelin had traveled to Arizona in August of 1877 with U.S. cavalry soldiers assigned to thwart Apache unrest. When Schieffelin audaciously announced he would head out on his own, the soldiers wished him well but scoffed, saying the only thing he was likely to find in the unstable area was his own tombstone. Undaunted, Schieffelin moved on and in February 1878, found a ledge of silver ore. Remembering the soldiers' dire warnings, Schieffelin named

Carolyn Bauer

his claims the Tombstone and the Graveyard. Since there were no assayers near by, Schieffelin headed north to the Signal mine. His brother Al, then working at the Signal, scoffed at his brother's find until mine assayer Richard K. Gird confirmed the high value of his ore samples. Gird grubstaked the Schieffelin brothers, convincing them to form a three-way partnership. The trio returned to the claim to discover that the Graveyard excavation was only a nominal pocket of ore. Unfazed, Schieffelin nosed through the desert sage, chipping away at rocks with his clinking sample pick. He scooted across the parched wasteland, lobbing useless rocks back into the desert until he ferreted out a rich claim he would call the Lucky Cuss. Amazingly, the very next day, Ed Schieffelin, who seemingly could *smell* silver, sauntered into yet another huge deposit-- the mighty Toughnut. Schieffelin's mines, together with the nearby Contention and Grand Central lodes, produced millions. The town of Watervale sprang up briefly near the Lucky Cuss, but the townsite was soon moved to present-day Tombstone. Schieffelin, a respected citizen, lived comfortably during his short but vigorous 50 years. He is buried on a hill outside the town. A monument over his grave reads, "This is my Tombstone."

Many others found their tombstones in this brawling, wide-open settlement. Gambling, prostitution, and drinking were natural enterprises in a town which issued more than 100 liquor licenses in 1880 alone, and where 14 faro tables ran day and night. Raging fires brought Tombstone to its knees in June, 1881, and May, 1882, but twice it rose from the ashes. The town of 15,000 boasted a school of 250 pupils in the early 1880s. Respectable adults worried about criminals

Carolyn Bauer   CRYSTAL PALACE

seeking refuge in their community, and they sought an end to unchecked violence--often vigilante-style.

In Bisbee, to the south, five desperados swaggered into the Goldwater & Castenada General Store, killed four people, robbed the till, and disappeared into the desert. A posse led by saloon keeper John Heath chased and caught the killers. The outlaws were imprisoned in Tombstone's jail, but it was soon discovered that Heath was an accessory, attempting to lead the posse astray. He was tried and sentenced to life in prison. A mob from neighboring Bisbee, enraged by Heath's light sentence, stormed the jail, carried out Heath, and unceremoniously lynched him from a nearby telephone pole. When the other gang members were sentenced to swing, a Tombstone entreprenuer built a small grandstand near the scaffold, planning to sell tickets. The structure offended the sensibilities of Tombstone residents, who razed the seats the evening before the hanging. Admission was free.

Tombstone, an Historical Landmark, is on U.S. 80, 24 miles southeast of Benson. Historic Allen Street has been refinished, presenting a long avenue of false-front buildings. For photographers on alternate Sunday mornings, Allen Street is declared a no parking zone. Tombstone has preserved a bounty of historic sites including the old Cochise County courthouse, Boothill Cemetery just outside town, the Bird Cage Theatre, and the OK Corral.

Carolyn Bauer   IN THE RICH HILL DISTRICT

WEAVER - Yavapai County

Pauline Weaver's reputation as a superior military and civilian guide ranked him as one of Arizona's favorite sons. On one expedition beginning near La Paz and ending near Antelope Valley, Weaver, Maj. A.H. Peeples, Jack Swilling and a motley group of whites and Mexicans camped near newly christened Weaver Creek. In the morning, their horses were missing and several of the Mexicans scoured the nearby hills for the animals. The errant horses were found on a mesa surrounded by pebble-sized nuggets, and the rush to the Rich Hill District began. Weaver, first called Weaver Camp and Weaverville, was quickly joined by the new settlements of Octave and Stanton. But gold fever held no lure for Pauline Weaver, and he soon moved on.

As the town of Weaver developed into a thriving mining center, rock and wood structures replaced crumbling adobe. But with growth came crime. The region became a haven for criminals, and the upstanding residents soon left. But its gold was nearly exhausted, and before the turn of the century, Weaver was absorbed into neighboring Octave.

Take the Stanton turnoff just north of Congress Junction on U.S. 89. Continue about a mile past Stanton. To the left of the dirt road sits an old rock powder house. On the hill above are haunting wood and rock skeletons of decaying buildings. The rocky area is home to rattlers, so caution is advised.

Thomas J. Barbre

WHITE HILLS - Mohave County

Relentless sheets of water and debris tore into the main shaft of the African mine on August 5, 1899 and 200 trapped miners ran blindly for the safety of side tunnels. On the desert floor above, the settlement of White Hills was also being devastated by the ferocious downpour. White Hills water usually cost $1 a barrel, but that day, said the *Mohave County Miner*, "we had a million dollar bath."

White Hills was established on this flat plain at the foot of the White Hills in 1894. Hualapai Jeff had shown miner Henry Shaffer some silver ore found near a red oxide deposit used as decoration in the Hualapai tribal ceremonials. The Hidden Treasure mine was discovered there, and the surrounding hills were soon crawling with prospectors. White Hills quickly grew to 1,500 residents. An English concern bought the new mining company and constructed a monstrous 40-stamp mill. By 1900 the mines had yielded millions in silver and gold and had no more to give. Production slowed, then ceased. Hardy residents hung on, but the White Hills post office was discontinued August 15, 1914.

Take U.S. 93 about 50 miles northwest of King-man. White Hills is five miles east of U.S. 93. There are few remnants of the once bustling town; all frame structures are rotting into the desert.

Carolyn Bauer　　　　WICKENBURG SCHOOL

WICKENBURG - Maricopa County

In the mid 1880s young Austrian Heinrich Heintzel heard the siren song of "gold!" echoing across the Atlantic to Europe. Heintzel answered, immigrating to the U.S. and Americanizing his name to Henry Wickenburg. Once in Arizona's gold country, Wickenburg strode into the desert to hunt game. A loud "crack" brought a vulture plummetting to the desert floor. Where the vulture's broken body lay, Wickenburg found a rich projection of gold-laden quartz. Thus began the Vulture Mine.

After trying his own hand at mining, Wickenburg devised a plan to sell unmined ore for $15 per ton, leaving the mining and milling to the customer. Eventually Wickenburg sold four-fifths of the Vulture to Benjamin Phelps who set up a 20-stamp mill and developed the Vulture Company. The Vulture Company ultimately wrested a fortune in gold from the parched wasteland, and leant its name to the the nearby town of Vulture City. Thirteen miles away, Wickenburg was established along the banks of the Hassayampa River. Though Henry Wickenburg discovered the wealthy Vulture Mine and had a town named for him, he suffered great poverty when Phelps withheld his share of the profits. Distraught and penniless, Wickenburg shot himself with his Colt revolver.

Wickenburg, an easy drive north of Phoenix on U.S. 89, is now a thriving town of friendly residents, restored mining era buildings, and a pleasant museum. The Vulture Mine is being redeveloped by new owners.